NAMU

Making Friends
with a
Killer Whale

By Ronald M. Fisher

☐ BOOKS FOR YOUNG EXPLORERS
NATIONAL GEOGRAPHIC SOCIETY

Many kinds of whales live in the oceans.
Namu is a powerful killer whale.
Other whales are afraid of killer whales.
They are fierce animals with sharp teeth.

Namu is just a medium-size whale,
but his eye is about the size of your fist.
Each tooth is as big as a man's thumb.
Nobody knew how Namu would act around people.

One day, Namu
had a big surprise.
While swimming
in the Pacific Ocean,
he got tangled up
in the nets of some
salmon fishermen.

The fishermen were
as surprised as Namu.
Instead of salmon,
they caught a whale.
His high, black fin
stuck out of the water
as he looked for a way
out. Namu was named
after a nearby town
in Canada.

Killer whales swim
together in groups,
or packs.
Some of the whales
from Namu's group
swam around nearby,
waiting and watching.

The owner of
an aquarium in
Seattle, Washington,
bought Namu
from the fishermen.
Namu made the trip
to his new home
in a floating pen.

A lot of people
lined up on bridges
to watch Namu
pass underneath.
He was in a pen
pulled by a
tough little tugboat.

Some people worried about Namu
and wanted him set free.

Namu's new home was protected
by a big net.
Inside, he jumped and played
and swam around.

Namu weighed about as much
as a big schoolbus;
so when he jumped,
        he made a mighty splash.

His new owner made friends with Namu
by feeding him when he got hungry.
Namu had a whale-size appetite.
He could eat 400 pounds of salmon a day.

Can you imagine
eating as much as Namu?
If you had a stomach
as big as his,
you could eat a
thousand hamburgers
at one time.

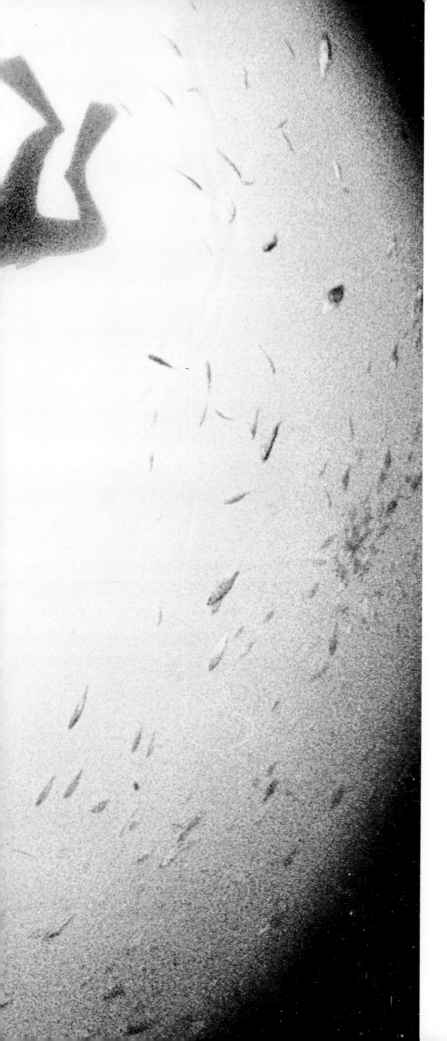

One day Ted Griffin,
Namu's owner,
jumped in the water
with the whale.
He wore a rubber
wet suit to keep warm
in the cold water.
Ted was afraid,
but he wanted to see
Namu up close.

Would Namu harm him?
Ted swam closer.
He touched Namu,
and fed him
a piece of salmon.
From that day on
they were friends.

Ted would stand up
in a little rowboat
to scrub Namu's back
with a long-handled brush.
Namu liked the scratching,
and he didn't want it to stop.

When Ted stopped,
Namu slapped the
water with his tail
and splashed Ted.

If Namu stayed too long on the surface of the water, his back would become sunburned.

In one quick bite
Namu could snap off
Ted's hand,
if he wanted to.

A killer whale has
about 50 teeth and
very powerful jaws.
Namu liked to have
people come swim
with him. He never
bit a friend.

Please help us
keep NAMU healthy

Scientists came to study Namu
to learn more about whales.
One scientist shot vitamins
into him with a bow and arrow.
Namu's coat of fat, called blubber,
was so thick he hardly felt it.

Scientists wanted to listen
to Namu's heart, and they used
a long pole to attach wires to him.
The wires were part of an instrument
to measure Namu's heartbeats.

First, one of the
scientists tried the
rubber cup on himself.
He wanted to make sure
it would stay in place
when they pressed it
against Namu. They
found that Namu's heart
beat fastest when he
was on the surface.

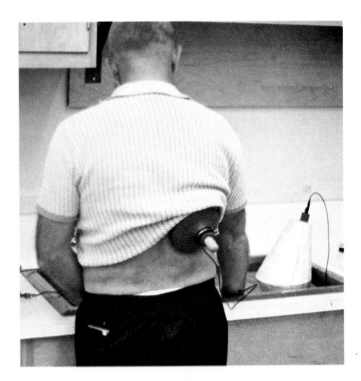

Glub
glub.
Even though whales live in water,
they are not fish. They are mammals,
and must breathe air just like people.
Namu breathes through a blowhole
on top of his head. He must come
to the surface to take a breath.

Air from Namu's blowhole
makes a trail of bubbles in the water.

Pilot Whale

Sperm Whale

Right Whale

Killer Whale

False Killer Whale

Whales live in all of the world's oceans.
There are 90 different kinds of whales.
Some whales have teeth. They feed on fish
and large sea animals. Other whales
don't have teeth, and they feed on tiny sea plants
and tiny sea creatures.

Humpback Whale

Bowhead Whale

Bottle-nosed Whale

Goose-beaked Whale

Pygmy Right Whale

Narwhal

Pygmy Sperm Whale

The blue whale
is the biggest animal
in the world.

The blue whale weighs
as much as 25 elephants.
His big tongue weighs
about as much as 40 men.

Ted went out in his little rowboat
to feed Namu salmon. Namu swam
under the boat. He's going to upset it.

he salmon fell out. Then he could have the fish all at once,

Namu let Ted ride
on his broad back.
He would swim
around his pen
while Ted held on tight
to the whale's high fin.

Sometimes Namu fell asleep
with Ted on his back.
Ted swatted Namu like a horse
to get him moving again.

In the water Namu was
as playful as a puppy with Ted.
He liked to roll over on his back
to have Ted rub his white belly.

Namu even swam on his back,
with his flippers in the air,
while Ted sat on his chest.
Best of all he liked the prize:
a big, tasty salmon.

Namu swims up
to the surface
for a big meal, and
to see the people
who have come
to visit him.
Everybody
        liked Namu.

Prepared by the Special Publications Division of the National Geographic Society

Melvin M. Payne, President; Melville Bell Grosvenor, Editor-in-Chief; Gilbert M. Grosvenor, Editor.

ILLUSTRATIONS CREDITS

National Geographic Photographers Bates Littlehales (1, 4-5 bottom), Victor Boswell and Robert S. Oakes (11), and James L. Amos (24-25); National Geographic Staff Andrew H. Brown (14-15, 19) and W. E. Garrett (31 bottom); Flip Schulke (2-3, 12-13, 16-17, 20-21, 26, 30-31, 32); Paul V. Thomas (4-5 top, 6 top, 7, 8-9, 10, 27 bottom); Ted Spiegel (6 bottom); Merrill P. Spencer (18, 27 top, 28-29, 31 top); Painting by Davis Meltzer (22-23).

Cover Photograph: Flip Schulke

Endsheets: E. N. Crain, Master Bookbinder, Colonial Williamsburg Foundation